TRUE HERESIES

Michael Daley

Červená Barva Press
Somerville, Massachusetts

Copyright © 2023 by Michael Daley

All rights reserved. No part of this book may be reproduced in any manner without written consent except for the quotation of short passages used inside of an article, criticism, or review.

Červená Barva Press

P.O. Box 440357

W. Somerville, MA 02144-3222

www.cervenabarvapress.com

Bookstore: www.thelostbookshelf.com

Cover Art: Cover photo: © Jay Mallin/ZUMA Press

Cover Design: William J. Kelle

Production: Allison O'Keefe

ISBN: 978-1-950063-63-5

Library of Congress Control Number: 2022942705

BOOKS BY MICHAEL DALEY

The Straits
The Dalmo'ma Anthology (ed.)
Angels
Yes: Five Poems
In Our Hearts & Minds: Anthology (ed.)
The Corn Maiden
Original Sin
Horace: Eleven Odes (tr.)
Rosehip Plum Cherry
To Curve
Way Out There
Moonlight in the Redemptive Forest
Alter Mundus by Lucia Gazzino (tr.)
Of a Feather
Born With
True Heresies
The Madrona Project (ed.)
Reinhabited: New & Selected Poems
Telemachus (a novel)

for our resistant spirit

ACKNOWLEDGEMENTS

Earlier versions of these poems first appeared thanks to:

Sing Heavenly Muse 1982 "Runner Up"
Waterways 1993 "Out the café window"
Kansas Quarterly 1993 "Saint Gabriel" "At the End of the World"
Off the Coast 2012 "Hinges & Splinters"
Rolling Thunder Review 2014 "Fling" "Listening to the Odyssey at 35000 Feet"
Greek Fire Anthology 2015 "A Jellyfish in the Company of Alcoholics"
Floating Bridge Review 2014 "Nothing Matters"
Switched on Gutenberg 2016 "Know Thyself"
Floating Bridge Review 2016 "Listening to the Odyssey at 35000 Feet"
Cirque 2017 "Undeniable"
Bozalta/Tierra Sagrada 2018 "The Revolution Shall Not Be Euthanized"
Samthology 2019 "Letter to Sam Hamill from Boston"
The Golden Walkman 2020 "The Martyrdom of Jamal Kashoggi"
Unlikely Stories Mark V 2020 "Soul of the World," "Relentless is the Order,"
      "Gift-Wrapped"
Prairie Schooner 2021 "Forgive the Market," "Outside the Inaugural Ball"

 Thanks to Mary Gillilan and Norman Green of *Clover, a Literary Rag,* for publishing several of my poems in the course of their sixteen issues between 2011 and 2019 including: "Tomorrow," "Face" "My Steamboat My Railroad My Horse" "Shall Seed the Wilting Not the Flower of Rose O My Metaphor" "I Think the World Is Falling Through a Void/ As Atoms Through My Flesh Make Time" "For I Will Consider My Truck, Ranger"

CONTENTS

1

Fling	3
Occupying Jesus	4
Face Like a Tide Pool Ear Like a Clam An Eye for the Limo	5
Shall Seed the Wilting Not the Flower of Rose O My Metaphor	6
Nothing Matters	7
Caricature of a Thin Face	8
Soul of the World	9
I Think the World Is Falling Through a Void as Atoms Through My Flesh Make Time	10
A Jellyfish in the Company of Alcoholics	11
He Was of the Clutch-Coat Generation	12
Listening to the Odyssey at 35000 feet	13

2

For I Will Consider My Truck, Ranger	17
State of the Union	18
Wing	19
Know Thyself	20
The Happiest Must Be Unable to Speak About Tragedy	21
Living It Out	22
They Are A People Who Live Entirely on Milk	23
The Revolution Will Not Be Euthanized	24
Oxalis	25
What You Said	26
At the Far End of Desire Lies a Kerchief Against the Wall	27
The Dispossessed	29

3

Undeniable	33
Elegy for the Fool	34
The Martyrdom of Jamal Khashoggi	35
Ozymandias Is My King	36
My Steamboat My Railroad My Horse	37
Woman with the Fat Arms	41
The Year of Our Retreat Comes Rudely to an End	42
Riding in the Back Cold, Nineteen-Seventy-Six, Stars Come Blown Down	43
Forgive the Market	44
Runner Up	45
Upright & Above Ground	46

4

Museum	49
Insomnia the Marriage of Days	50
Outside the Inaugural Ball	51
Hinges & Splinters	52
Letter to the County	53
Tomorrow	54
Face	55
Relentless Is the Order	57
After Reading Basho on Solstice at Shi Shi Beach During the Treasonous Reign of the Leper King	58
War Crimes	59

5

Revelatory	63
Hapless	64
In Defense of "Irony"	65
And Et Cetera	66
Burn Moon August Six Twenty-Seventeen	67
Take Five	68
Of Myself I Sing	71
Pharaoh's Dance	72
Letter to Sam Hamill from Boston	75
Lucretius, an Interpretation	78
Autobiography of the Last Monarch Butterfly	80

6

Cells	89
Teatime	92
Bird Count on Back Roads	93
1957, Paragon Park	95

Note
About the Author

"I have just suggested that the concept of alienation seems to become questionable when the individuals identify themselves with the existence which is imposed upon them and have in it their own development and satisfaction."

—Herbert Marcuse

"Poetry is society's heretic, and its auto da fé becomes the cherished goal of press and state. Its heresies are the songs sung at the barricades, forbidden songs that crack windows and walls and explode crystal."

—Djelloul Marbrook

TRUE HERESIES

1

It is not with the lyre of someone in love
that I go seducing people.
The rattle of the leper
is what sings in my hands.

—Anna Ahkmatova

Fling

No matter what they say they know, it wrecks us that they do.
Twelve sainted years she spoke out, then hit with a piece of steel,
her wisdom was a blur. Nietzsche's compassion
to protect the horse from the whip, but he was already gone.
Wright in the saguaro, less biography and we'd know "Duffy's Hammock."
The noble and the romance heave above a seawall and everybody knows.
Our two neighborhood barflies: the photo caught them—
their teeth, their tipped hats—fools, we thought.
When she arrived in those boots, we saw it was time to go.
At that abandoned shack the reluctant hay farmer said no children
keep them boards over them holes in the ground. They started in the loft,
though she'd marked him earlier at the pool table in blue chalk.
Then at a hut by the bay naked in iced high tide to their waists,
he longed for dawn. Twice at the empty house beside the transformer,
it hummed B Flat over whiskey, sweat, and ache.
And on cars, in the back of a pickup, in field mud once,
high on a ridge by campfire flapjacks,
at the small funnel of a boat hull on a mat: on crackers and itch.
The breakfast waiter with the red mustache and Chicago accent,
his laugh at them crackling in his chest, said they smelled like no sleep,
like fuck, like the love of one's body under a knuckle of the other's.
One of them at the door to the tavern said *That's it* and got away.

Occupying Jesus

"Everybody must get stoned"

Had you been a young man in the B.C.E.,
would you have stoned the saints?
Would you have stoned the martyrs who abide, and the faithful?
Would you stone to the ground the True Believer?
Who gets to pass through Gates of Empire unscathed by lions or lambs?
The marbles in my cheek taught me to speak like a grown man,
but when I spat them out, how could I help but strike you,
noble lover of optimism spurned beside the fountain's plume?
Oh, come closer that I might bite thee!
The fear of the cross withered at the beachside grave.
Can't we escape it? You would have been that story-telling gypsy
who heisted the extra nail aimed at the heart
and I the frustrated legionnaire who groveled all over for it
only to smirch my spear-tip with savior blood.
I might have wept but the spill of blood turned the Golgotha gold,
and, good tinkers, we went off to peddle it.

Face Like a Tide Pool, Ear Like a Clam, an Eye for The Limo

The sun a crisp peel off your legs and back as from a canvas by the mighty artist,
a national treasure you drop in the street, the torso doubles as an ornament.
Hang it from the red barn door where the faulty hide can dry.
Wear the cap and gown to bed, cave dweller among rhetoricians.
The window is open, a spider up a wooden table sits and waits
for the child in an "oh" of sleep to let himself down the braid,
spin round legs as antennae on rooftops twist and climb a pale sea.
Cake crumbs under the skin produce a rhino's disposition,
everybody following the giraffe who spots danger fastest.
Me knowing you has been better than paychecks arriving,
and butter on the tongue. You were the jewel
on the glimmering lip ring and in pain we're singing we
love you, Sugar Cup, licensed to bear alabaster for Cleopatra's parade.

Shall Seed the Wilting Not the Flower of Rose, O My Metaphor.

Stars and planets float into order and chaos
where the lifted finger, as sand in the garden,
a pattern of change, points to migrants and settlers.
The planted foot, a tide eroding the rule of number,
in luck and heartbreak, signals design or choice.
In the wish for atonement will and despair
change sorrow to lightning, iodine to hope.
Charm without smiling. But the smile to disarm greets peace.
The blood and the semen, borrowed and honored,
followed and scorned by love of division
for substance and matter. Hope without atoms
is a reckoning of wills, a freckle on the collarbone,
skull of a baby, birth of the arrowhead,
the trouble with husbands taken for granted.
The uses of bubbles go out with the tide.
Ship out on star light far from this channel, gift of the graces.

Nothing Matters

There are atomic numbers in my bones.
Hair electric, of thee I sing.
Pressure on the plates of memory
so traces of the, impulse of the, sheer refracted
shadow of the once-walked-here
found in the curl you let fall in slumber,
memory of your body twilit once along a street,
cigarette scent cool of the evening
balmy sidewalk, all from that atom
once traversed a magnitude of one in motion.
Take this plume of light to a pool from whence,
in iron infinity, gush seeds of things in seas of nothing.

Caricature of a Thin Face

Would have fell in love, would have fell,
but the nascent moon wasn't having it.
A face crackled under these thumbs,
under knuckles, eyes shut anyway—
but how far must I go to hide behind them?
We shriveled midgets, tribe of wallowers,
toters, and knaves, who somebody knees
in the theater in the dark with a message
sniveled over a paper, then recedes in flip flops
down the dry compartments of fever-driven train cars.
Writhe while you can, Nosferatu,
clip back the tiny hedge in your will
and take to the dance floor standing tall.
It might end in an air of blame
or, worthiness aside, we could tree the wild cat,
and fleece the hunter raw.

Soul of the World

A silhouetted man, a small yellow flame in his chest,
chops a snake to wriggling sectors
which turn the ghosts of heads to lick or bite his hand.
Guillotined heads kept together in burlap bags
were found to have bitten rather than kissed
one another's cheeks; a body flopping
along the guillotiner's large platform
reminded the history teacher of a chicken
in his neighbor's back yard, World War Two,
in search of its obnoxious personality or soul if there is one
for hunger, lust, mothering soft-boiled eggs, hatred of pecking, impatience
for her turn at the taste of meal,
or hierarchic complaints to the Spiritus Mundi Chicken
bottled up till you took the cap off.
That nameless thing, the spirit of the whole spirit,
sculling in its little shell, its subatomic prow upon the river,
gets the soul drunk—who knows what's more enduring than wine—
my eyes closed, the doors nailed shut.

I Think the World Is Falling Through a Void
As Atoms Through My Flesh Make Time

The gods are invisible, but into whose soup
was this straitjacket dropped, fourth century BC?
Euclid tosses the textbooks out a window
smashes them with axes beribboned
simply to square the loom.
His mind moving at ninety-three set a course.
Empirical verities shrink in the shadow of number.
Pythagoras, of course, of the golden thigh,
who never sat upon a can of beans,
plunking the strings or hammering out a toneless ringing
as they did around Samos in the blacksmith's yard.
Octaves, fifths, fourths, the imperfect tone half-split.
A locomotive chugging through the centuries the fear of gods.
Now we have only the One.
The teacher puts his hands on you to make the truth appear:
"A crisis of foundations!
Look, having discovered incommensurables,
he and all aboard perished in shipwreck..."
and Aristotle went on sniffing his apple to stay alive.

A Jellyfish in the Company of Alcoholics

Who said because atoms conceive of a source
necessity causes chance, unmortals mortals,
destruction generation, and antimatter matter?
Curses are prayers and Aquinas' Blesseds
had a window on Hell to swell their ecstasy.

Yet Alcibiades was drunk before sailing to war
and smashed the bust of Hermes.
Called back from the Gulf to testify,
his Greeks of course were defeated.

At that collegium heads never mind chairs rolled
if they opposed the state-owned gods.
Yesterday a preacher marched into the classroom,
pinched a student's ear and dragged him out.

Who would throw himself upon the fire
to save the other ear? How many intellectuals
are throwing punches tonight in bars
and for whose version of freedom?

He Was of the Clutch-Coat Generation

Thieves in the Basilica,
salami-munchers wandering in the rear pews,
the *scuola cantorum* aflame singed
to its turquoise roots the ruined vocabulary
of the voluptuous minute of adolescence.

Language is tied to every atom.
Syntax of a species under the hood
is a throbbing molecular pattern.

Still experimenting with the body, checking her teeth,
the well-dressed Euro-teen on the train platform
sniffs her armpits.

Listening to the Odyssey at 35000 feet

I drift into a grove
where a three-sided sculpture
is nearly complete.
The fourth side wraps like a glove,
its red crinkled texture,
flesh turned inside out.

The robes of the world grow dark
far from the stallion land of Argos
and the awful reek of those sea-fed brutes.

*And he chased her over the hill and down,
in leaves, in soft grasses,
she with her arm band and leather string for a crown,
until he tackled her where she started up the hill.
She was smiling.*

Pouring the lustral water,
he scattered the barley meal.
The heifer wrapped in gold foil,
slashed her throat for barbecue.

*A crystal in the broken shoe,
everything you've ever wondered stepped on.
Calypso not waving from the beach,
this is the hallowed bier
from which she last viewed him
without a ripple in sight, clear sky,
the grass mistakenly graced by departure,
feather set in the sand drops a shadow at three.*

And in the background,
over headphones, screaming children, hungry
deep-voiced men laughing,
a whole section of the poem
must be moved "off to the side."

On his way the father, though sickly,
his cancer advanced, made a stop
at the small black house
of someone he did not know
and removed a large beige animal
by dragging its hind quarters
across the carpet for the creature was heavy, formless
but round and appeared
to have come up from the sea.

2

*Oh, what quenchless feud is this that Time
hath with the sons of men*

—Herman Melville

For I Will Consider My Truck, Ranger

For he can creep.
—Christopher Smart

That it be metaphor to meadows
That the dull tooth cut through reality precise and slow
That it clatter
That its rivetless undercarriage complain at idle
      and the bespectacled shalt turn in rigs on high
          impeccably appointed for a haul of sun to services blocks away
That it stand without charge guiltless and indifferent
That at cable it leap to the mouse of spark
That my own fingers cause to ignite
That it float on bald under-filled balloon synthetics of jungles
      till blowouts out of cell range on back country hick log-spurs
      and it sag without blame, regret or expectation on limp headlamps
That it is emotionless causality my touch ignites
That my musculature twist its interlocked geometries,
      unspeakable bearings, greasy tranny, squeaking linkages
      and slippy clutch foot pedal
That it abide by the map in my head though faulty while I,
      skeptic of Google, refuser of gas pump direction pointers,
      blind Oedipus sweating out the doom,
      take my life to back roads in far places
That it be spear for conquest
That the thumb ignite
That puddles of unplumbed fossil be war, though Peace sticker its bumper
That its cause of causes rattles on like unfed grandma in the ward
That every direction sets mountains of odes on odometer free

State of the Union

Wires inside the target muscled there by welders
whose faces wear the strain
of so many bombs fraught with our anatomy
spit out by the Constitution as if we
however we designate our split personalities
crow from garbage bins and paste together
our salutary offerings from the high wire of love.
We walk with brooms through these beaten streets
and wipe away courage from the eyes of children
and we know the deck of cards we used
loaded with misinformation and unforeseen chance
will not give us the means to wind our watch
let alone take the salt and pepper pit-bull
down the sidewalk for our evening's constitutional.
In all weather we permit ourselves to exercise this right
so ecstatically we can't repeal it
and we vote along as if it matters
calling out blasphemies of opinion
and little diamonds of insight, mattering
if only to our own mothers, but mattering
that we say it that we think it that
we want it, that we were here.

Wing

Wing backward and forward, wing in the dark.
Hallucinatory, captured bird, prey of domestic cat,
skull of the one in flight, torn wing hung north.

By this compass you guess the way home,
heal the breach in nature, fix the fiction
up where Orion's singing, buckle and flute to the world.

Settle back, the space age is a minute of history,
an eyelash of time. Crowds bus up to Venus
and leave the middle class behind.

We paid through the nose to stop by the Sea of Tranquility,
so, fuck you, Buck! Kiss my ass, Flash!
Nighttime sky looms in our headlights.

Know Thyself

If one's dog were the embodiment of one's soul,
mine is this off-putting, snippish hermaphrodite.
Nobody knows but she how impossible is the moon's stillness.
Nobody can follow a trail with as much snoutish superiority.
Her story is that of a ship battered on a wild coast
whose crew washes up on a beach and christens it Paradise.
With such small paws my selfless soul issues forth,
protectress of any sand where my shadow might pass.
She argues and assails and quivers endlessly
as if a reunion with the double were imminent,
long lost stray and careless littermate who bolted downwind
after an unpleasant seagull and never came home.
She is gigantic in her own so-called mind, a thing
itself like my own half-aware skeptic's etch-a-sketch,
blank as impotence, impaired by mortal blindness.
She is that noble eminence I see every day in the mirror,
much too self-consoled to need any smoothing hand
along my hackles, fur raised in an instant to protect you
who so kindly has a biscuit in your pocket even now if I behave.

The Happiest Must Be Unable to Speak about Tragedy

The girl in the back
says let's let the diseased help
control the population and don't
soften the pain unless it's the cure.

Thirteen-year-old survivalist raised
by Salvationists.
Others question did she ever suffer loss.
Had a cure been available
in the Great Flu pandemic of 1918,
could the body rags draped over a cart
have influenced her, as ethicist in charge
of limiting the population,
to offer it?

Living It Out

This is how first people made movies.
They touched the sky with both hands, threaded
light through a hive and pictures of you
doing things you never did appeared,
questions you never thought twisted on your thumb,
thread dropped in the honey jar,
that sticky continuum, a film in the whirlpool,
a stone electric truth inescapable as mahogany
zooms in as your fugitive car flees
their cameras behind the cold stars.

They Are a People Who Live Entirely on Milk

"They sit perpendicular to rock face
as two of their diviners plunge
hundreds of feet into a milky pool."

Herr Reichmann loves ceremony,
follows it globally as sport.

"They think that the moon
is the place to be
and pine for it."

"Only idiots or artists worship purity,"
sewing into the bag the diver's cadaver.

"You claw your way to the milk.
Rebirth! Hobble along then.
Get you gone.
Butter if you tarry."

The Revolution Will Not Be Euthanized

Saw Captain Mortimer from the old ship who was looking out for me,
big out-of-work guy in a white shirt on a bench beside the door.

A brotherhood of metal on metal, wood on wood,
of a class of men who get up to work and exhaust their bodies.

Much too fast come the discouraged dreams, sweeping my face like fish—
Do I see this? Am I listening? Do I believe?

How can I be so peaceful? I go along and remain unprovoked.
I ease back out of conscious choices—

> *Sing to me, Morty.*
> *Are you asleep within pale*
> *arms and dust?*

Night supervises significant dilemmas, overrides
urgings of conscience.

The day's light exposes a shame so common it gives me peace,
but not peaceable, no. No, not pacified. How can I think that?

I was never a young mind refreshed by lawlessness, or vanquished
by free will, my canoe will not overturn in the rushing stream.

Oxalis

One of my chickens has fallen in love with the visiting poet.
He must sit on the creaky front porch, in the rocker,
where he has lifted the chicken up
and holds her delicately in his arms
as she flaps her once indolent wings
near his aging, tolerant face.
She is gray as a pigeon and has lived as a morose bird,
feathers scraggly from weeks and months she hasn't lain.
He's exasperated, but patient.
She's kissing him. Yes, a chicken
with its nasty pecking beak,
kissing our friend the celebrated poet,
her wings fluffed, a gray mystical helter-skelter of love
flapping about his head. It turns out, or so he explains,
she is one of his girlfriends reincarnated
who had nothing to live for, who didn't know she was a chicken,
didn't remember she loved a poet, and music, was oh so happy.
When she does allow him to attend to other duties,
she remains perched on the rocking chair,
her eyes two squints of pure joy.
Suddenly two potted plants on the rotting porch change color.
Stems and leaves go from pale white to a lustrous green.
It's as if the colorist of a grand cartoon flushed each
with bright health, as if the wand of a magician
had swept their whole length.
When chickens are happy, apparently,
a contagion sings among the oxalis.

What You Said

And I want to know, Thalia, what, if anything, I had to offer someone so cold, so callous, I mean, or—let me just be as really catty as I can for the moment (I'm sure you won't mind; after all, who but you and I will ever hear this claptrap anyway?

Excepting, of course, Raoul—but does he count? As a legitimate reader, I mean? As critic? As orphaned ingénue adrift on an intellectual raft somewhere where you and I,

My noble walrus, are mere cabin cruisers honking flatulently in the night?)— catty as I can be, that is, toward you, you vindictive slut, you small-mouthed bigot, you over-zealous missionary of a church no god would have the temerity to accept collections from—you grease-chinned heiress of the mud factory.

You daughter of bad breath and crushed cigars—you are the sole reason for my latest fiasco, my doom caused by your duplicitous sliminess which also sent poor hapless Raoul into spasms

And who knows what-all after the bloodthirsty lobotomizers get through with him or did you even know, you spit-sucking, throat-clearing liar?

At the Far End of Desire Lies a Kerchief Against the Wall

1.
A breeze left it, postage stamp on a glossy card.
Scribble on the back, "I love you from the sea
the sea by the beautiful sea."
Calling from the entrance to a cave,
love inhabited by Roman conquerors.
Contempt is a glove in the chilblain cold.

2.
Her troubled mother reaches through the phone
to an ear, human, not accusing,
"What she wrote was not true...
a girl in a hurry to get in step,"
thoughtful face on the incoming tide, weed
in her hair and her ears,
daughter molested by, touched, dreaming . . .
the one she let in by the front door.
On the intake of breath: " . . . Abuse. Yes,"
Life goes on swings Ringo in the parlor
as she switches the phone to the other ear.
The cast uncomfortably fits her wrist.

3.
And on the song went,
trippingly off the throat of the singer aspurt on Holofernes' slab.
His cankerous, wanderlust, scabrous moon
descends over a desert ridge,
scraping his sword on the gravel.
He willed the breaking snowmelt in the highway,
a honeyed heat wave over the oaten fields,
the biblical chaos of landslides,
this crude calculus of his conscious will.

4.
The piping of his shirt torn
as if by the narrator's own two hands,
he strove, Captain Lullaby,
to iron out the problem,
the love instrument pealed above her head.
The ranks of the dead are strengthened
by our names proclaiming the good,
Calypso's body draped on the beach as his sails unfurl.

The Dispossessed

On the tooth of a sea rock, rip tide swallowed a city.
Walls hung rumors. There was no wind,
only those green walls, and hunched jackals.

Lost student days, we drank in the postcard light.
We raided the courtyard or had our iced tea on the shore.
Our typed pages drifted far from the lounge chair.

Then came the wind. Dawn clanged at the windowpane
where our breath moistened, and evaporated,
where the brittle lips of widows chafed.

Frost caressed the juniper in a photo of some silky daybreak.
That pointy headed one of us, bent like questions,
his tracks on wet pavement, who spoke for him?

Given enough time, happy man, he could have
beaten wings like a fearless bird at the lip of a hill,
and filled his lungs with shards of those important days.

Afterwards, we had no thought where to meet.
By the broken rock? Beside the beached hull?
If we get there, we said, we'll sing like a willing drum.

3

From my five arms and all my hands,
From all my white sins forgiven, they feed

—Philip Levine

Undeniable

Typhoon follows hurricane
follows flood follows drought is not
the probable course of nations
in decayed branches
songbirds attached

Raving lunatics will not
farm out the cold sea's
metaphysical purity
Shall not pick the lock
to burning Arctic summer

Elegy for the Fool

The challenge is to utter its name sincerely
The challenge is a hope beyond the predictable
The challenge is space
The challenge is abundance in senility
The challenge is become who you already were
    to name the challenge the challenge
The challenge is no romantic glove, but a worn hide tossed down,
    no slap across a cheek
The challenge is five eagles above the windy lichen
    whirring out of small waves
The challenge is a stolen walk in flood grass clumps
    on a trail turned stream
        past the illegal yokel duck hunters' guffaws & gunshots
The challenge is soft, is manly, camouflaged in a brave day
The challenge is innocence
The challenge is shore birds alone, the distance filled with sea
The challenge becomes blindness
The challenge is offended by tactile cowardice,
    rage of a poet on a rock in the wind
The challenge turns to mud on a Monet afternoon
The challenge is a cathedral there is no surviving, a challenged
    god in a landscape with saxifrage
The challenge is sweet to the tongue and to sing it to sing it like a fool
    with hopeless signs—the family's living in a car
The challenge is frugal, and he died of overdose
The challenge is a safety net parked below a moral footprint
The challenge is to believe, o pure product of America,
    not in the no one who drives the car,
            but in speaking love's name with the eyes

The Martyrdom of Jamal Khashoggi

When I punch a hole in my timecard
at the door to the weapons parlor
where fuselage, spear, tongue of defender
click for the kingdom of the pure
whose wealth we reckon with thumbprints
on triggers we're proud to instill,
our steel facility is cleansed by his name.
We'll name some ordnance for his arm,
an arsenal just for his heart,
sharpshooters learn the coil of his eye.
His tongue steeps in acid tea brewed from dollars,
his giant face crawls through the world
on haunches of a beast behind children
in a wildflower hologram, ghastly evacuees
from clouds we fabricate, genocide babies,
their eyes like our own were in childhood—
that same dismay—though now
we have jobs, holy martyr, you could kill,
and parts of you we bag and purify
and spread through the meadow where flowers
spring up in my name and in your name.

Ozymandias Is My King

Morning breezes tremble the ash. In blackberry root balls,
in a towhee's song, in water-throated redwing's,
I built a massive fire pit primal as any flag.

I pried stone after stone with an iron bar, lugged them all,
drenched in old man's heart sweat and turf decay.
Today those skewed rocks orbit some burnt sticks.

Blackberry shoots looped the last owner in his pajama cuffs
when they found him down in chicken coop soil, rich in lime and rust.
He tilled nails and shards of blackberry wine into the garden.

So did his wife, that harridan. She cleaned fish, skinned his rabbit.
He knew and so do I, one season's fruity weed devours a sour acre,
will eat up my stonework. Their juicy stems already grapple the ash.

My Steamboat My Railroad My Horse

Vivir y Beber
—Hugo Hiriart

Across the conference table smooth dark hands
of the one-time medical student
shoot like lizards over a dry stone.
"What a greasy dawn"—when his night shift ended
at ghoulish *Hospital del Sagrat Cor*,
and he boarded the *Begoña*, from
Barcelona to Havana with no
goodbye.

"*Señor*—Mister—we're not just another Mexican
working the Brussels sprouts." We wandered off
the topic—his grandson Fausto, my student,
who was proud to be reading *Don Quixote*.

If you observed us, from across the reverberant hall,
we'd look like accomplices:
two nodding, white-hair geezers, hatching escape.
Or ghosts—of parent-teacher nights—
years I cajoled kids who translated, maybe accurately,
for their respectful parents across tables
the School District arrayed, an institutional gesture.

This one, the grandpa, had a story, had the past.
Casino dealers—Father Confessors,
bartenders in state capitals,
hunger for stories as good.
For me he describes the air the day his train
chugged out of Vera Cruz:

"Like when you run through a yard—
your face molds to a wet sheet
on the clothesline.
A river ran along the track,
we slithered by the bank.

"What I left you can't understand.
And when I left, I left.
I didn't exchange goodbyes with Maricela, decadent
Maricela, her green gown
haunts me, her excuse always the same:
'*Tu sabes como yo bebo,*' and then she hugs me.
She was an artiste, our chanteuse.
She dispensed silly surrealist proverbs:
'... *meaning is beneath the letters.*
The 'I' goes upstairs.
That's why symbolism works; it's Morse Code.'

"Marta, her twin, in purple dress of a sheer fabric,
turns her back, but says to me, '*Faustinado?*
Tu sabes como yo vivo,' nods at the dark green specter
of a smear below Maricela's eyes
when she drops her narrow mask,
a swag of velvet on a spindling shaft,
she grips between her finger and thumb.

"I had on the black hat of travel.
Marta, with her skinny 'crustacean shoulders,' disappeared among
the cocktails and smoke.
Years later, in the city of Guanajuato,
she accepted to marry me—Fausto's her *nieto*.

"Why did I marry her? Are you kidding? Maricela—
she drives up to my house before dawn,
crawls through a window,
she throws a knife at my door.
I left. I left all of it.
But never have I tired of loving My Marta.

"Maricela spoke so cruel I should have known
she didn't want forgiveness.
I was trapped, she was a captive.
She'd say, '*What does she expect?*
The Bitch has boobs like punctured inner tubes.
I won't live long enough to please her.
I'll be an apparition soon.'

"I wept that last evening—
I remembered as I dismounted the mare
all sweating on some peak, and, I thought, stared at
the Pacific, but I was mistaken—
that was the Sea of Cortez.

"Next morning, she lost her key again,
and I was far away.
She searched my every pocket,
had my pants brought
from the dry cleaners:
on the subway
she had tossed
an open bottle—
'*You should have known.*
I always throw the corks away.'

"The key not in any pocket
even the tiny pocket inside the
pocket where I forget coins
and, surprised on good days,

drop them
in the tip jar—"
              "But" I interrupt,
"let's talk about your grandson
who reads *Don Quixote,*"
and of whom
I'm very proud
he got jumped out
of Norteños,
though they shot his toes.

"He'll never work fields like me.
Or Marta. I know—you've heard before:
we're slaves to get the kids out.
Our trouble is we want so much—
our meaning is beneath what you know.

"When I left, I left—by steamboat, by railroad, by horse.
I sat on a rocky ground.
In my gray valise I found her metal key,
cold to touch, in dust and crumbs of cake,
I tied it to a stone and hurled it in a mountain lake."

Woman with the Fat Arms, Somerville, 1980

After the heat wave, Sunday's rain strikes
the kitchen screen so hard
drops filter through and drive the coleus crazy.

She's waiting for the Captain,
who works nights at the fire.
She listens for her children,
as the rain freckles her arm.

They're peeking in a window
at young neighbors beneath a sheet
undulant as sea kelp.

She pillows her face in her arm, her lips wet.
Rain was a happy voice, but hers strains
in Portuguese the children hate.

Thirteen in the sand with the Captain.
Her father the fisherman told how he wept.
Estremadura's a corpse for me now!

She was a baby, he held her up for neighbors,
rain on his face. If she entered Lisboa,
would Isabel remember? And Niño, would he?

Her father's a breeze to flutter a curtain.
She opens the screen, her arms rest on the sill.
She leans out past the aluminum frame.

The Captain never stoops beside tomatoes.
Fire trucks all night. Over drooping three-deckers,
there's a smudge of rain, a shout in the street.

The phone goes off next door.
Rain prints her black skirt.
She listens for the children.

The Year of Our Retreat Comes Rudely to an End

In winter, a shroud over this our native foreign country,
we roam without discretion into rooms we shouldn't enter.
Each day a shudder, and perform our duty,
wrinkles washed in early rain, late premonitions,
the bell we keep hearing—anxious a month before songbirds.
When did time passing, any time, ever please us?

No one departs without warning: this year or next
has a black month around which whirl the tin fairies frilled
in the wind-tangled chimes. Cast into a stream,
the legendary fishhook spools off warnings like a pleasure boat
deep-sixing champagne, corks bobbing in our wake,
rocking ourselves to sleep in the hold, unlucky,
stinking of catch we'll toss overboard in the morning.

Riding in the Back, Cold, 1973, the Stars Come Blown Down

Last night's stars come down in dust-filled pickup trucks,
downhill at fifty, come off the roof like snakes
and come down the motorless wind
turned to pearls falling from a plate.
Last night the sky in the door of a truck,
some tree-root, and a lean star in the blasted house,
a wheel hanging in a tree,
and the driver singing,
the driver of a hard diamond
that whines in a fluted cloud, spits
at the buckshot sky.

in memory, Rusty North

Forgive the Market

> *I renounce the blindness of the magazines.*
> —James Wright

I have lost the habit.
A yellow-jacket and a leaf bother my head.
I fold my hands.
A puff of breeze builds the world.
The white mare whinnies and sweeps her tail.
Her broad horse's ass vanishes in the stream.

Runner Up

Lana Woluski, whom I've loved since first grade,
is standing across the dance floor with the other girls
on prom night of our junior high school graduation.
She looks at me, her eyes sparkling, wide with tears.
Her face glowing, she appears almost ecstatic.
And bounds across the room toward me, arms flung out,
radiating new love. Then my best friend, Billy Dame,
steps forward and she plunges into his arms.
I look away, their shadows gleam on the floor.

Upright & Above Ground

> *Life gradually and imperceptibly glides into old age and succumbs,*
> *not to a quick assault, but to a long-continued siege.*
> —Cicero

I'm bent to the dirt, a sunless mirage
bleeds into my early risings,
and aging reappears. I'm lucky:
language hides nothing—
aging only seems to tick off seasons,
to slacken the bowstring
that once shot me across time.
Yet, worn to a dull blur,
inexcusably unapologetic,
I fade to an absurdity,
to bits you could shake out:
clunky hips, brittle pacemaker,
hammered will, a self,
but pills of light spark my palms,
every muscle wrenched just to be.

4

Heretics banged at the double door.

—Natalie Diaz

Museum

Moths whose petals in wing
behind glass avoid dust
line the west wall
dripping down a canvas.
Outside, the light wells
beneath the streetlamp,
beneath the bulb
securing I'm the target
on the stage which spins
around the silk
moth, a goddess who
crouches over to
draw from her own vagina
a silken webbing,
the metaphysical cocoon,
where beside the fetus jar,
a hieroglyph on wing
points the way.

Insomnia, the Marriage of Days

The retired trapezist loops a hand around her husband's wrist.
A day begins. Left arm, right leg come up through sand.
To be reminded—the body is its own possession
and "all my worldly goods do I on thee bestow."
The moon at three was on the roof and then awash in the wading pool,
and sliced across the white lace curtain, dressed for night or day.
Blue sky, hot for days and days, stretch your bruised hands to me.

Outside the Inaugural Ball

All the grieving
      sounds
            in public malls and
on the cracked sidewalks where
weeds freeze now

plastic wrappers
      fly by

      Who has the time
to petition the government to
reclaim its humanity

The beloveds
      in every household
            are leaving us behind in
the middle of the parking lot,
      the temperatures plunging into
            minus

Hinges & Splinters

The builder called a home organic
and banned us from remodeling.
Home, he says, is a system tangled in systems

and lots more hip metaphor
for all the rooms we occupy,
we the seven billion remodelers.

And that's only humans.
How many ants, and elephants,
what weeds shoulder through pavement.

The year began at a railroad crossing
and I was happy, uplifted
by my resolution: Stand up more.

Science, our tool to fix cluttered wiring,
plumbing, to learn balance,
says stand and live longer.

Then a mile of coal cars, a recitative,
rolled its dirge downtown.
I felt that twinge grind inside.

I called it "fear." It echoed in my skull
as I walked uphill,
along the shoulders of the world,

tapped my doorframe into place,
and I was home.

Letter to the County

The debate is property versus water
and nobody wins

A fly or two circles
where the tea water sloshed
under an Easter sunburst

Three murmuring hummingbirds
jockey for the sugar water
and overshoot the border
of our little plot

I can't hold back the glacier
with a vote

Tomorrow

I've forgotten how to grip my fat black pen.
It slips around, spongy in my fingers.

A pen born to leak genius, it forgets glyphs
I shaped from an ink well
in Miss Nealy's dim first grade.

Palmer method embalmed—
drowned in curlicue river eddies—
the map along my palm hides hills,
embankments, fields where deer browse.

Down the heel in sloping grass blades
I find newborn lambs springing
and a fence, and a sheep dog,
and a flea rises up, nuisance
of gnawing simplicity I miss so.

Fingers callous, the awkward scratch a hen
claws over my dirty mind.
I cough, dust lifts above lime,
my pen going wild in the barn
to leak milk from a stone,
if the sun allows, tomorrow.

Face

Beauty
Faces need to be measurable
to give meaning beyond the rumpling
of flesh, to express intimacy
within the interruption of our talk.

Your mouth turns down means mystery,
your brow lifts, the answer.
The day moth flutter across your lip,
an unrehearsed animal
as clean as a lavender petal
tipped to the rain.

Persona
This act, both comedy and tragedy,
of the little man far below our seats
up here on the cliff worn white by Greek sun,
holding up his grand mask to witness
truth like roulette—and the bullet has our number.

The face a hidden poker hand,
the man superior to us covers his mouth
the way a flirtatious stranger does, bus full of eyes,
stage furniture hammered in a dream.

Innocence
The face before it experiences a self
floats through traffic.
It is a mussel facing the sea,

as yet unharmed by tides.
Or a novel held too close to the eye.

Yet once asked, the self rides shotgun
and weathers like a shell
from the tedium in waves.
It is as if two massive palms
held both sides and slowly pressed,
or the covers of a slim book gently, irrevocably,
closing on far too many pages.

Relentless Is the Order

Queued in our stockings and socks before TSA,
its familiar mechanism for scrutiny enfolds us—we meek, we patient,
we mild jokesters for whom officers pretend ease as ice gazes
appraise old photos, beardless visages—familiar too
the uniform memorialized instructions wrung above a human hum
conveying our luggage, our wealth, icons, joys, our meds, odd shoes.
We rush—we meek, we halt, we limp, we pissed, we ordered
in this primal relationship—bag-lugging queue and guard,
a comfort in a way, willingly to herd behind the gesture:
enter the device, valuables belong here, pockets shall be empty.
When did this begin? Was there a border to cross with our immigrant
impurities into Egypt? A line of soiled beseechers and attendants
at the Emperor's gates subject to pat down? Who's to say whether
with our smeared passports, we meek, we loving innocents arrive
at divine gates scanned by wand, humbled to exhausted tears,
the child led away by stranger's fingers, as we step into the next
line, we travelers eternal, inured, in shock, we wait.

After Reading Basho on Solstice at Shi Shi Beach During the Treasonous Reign of the Leper King

I found a long black feather
and combed out the wet sand, bits of shell.
An eagle dropped it
into a nearly empty stream bed
where a fleet of gulls, merry gulls,
strew the remains.

War Crimes

> *Society is like a stew. If you don't stir it up every once in a while,
> then a layer of scum floats to the top.*
> —Edward Abbey

The Senator was protecting, like a she-bear,
that revered Dr. K., who, at ninety-one and invited
to advise the Senate subcommittee, was wheeled
past protesters, a Greek Chorus chanting names
of countries where Henry's legacy arose,
where countless human animals boiled in
or fled our poisons, our strafing,
boots we crept in to make them safe.
When they chanted the name, "Vietnam,"
the Senator cried out. Once, I had assumed
he spoke with my own heart.
I lied to myself that he knew the city streets,
could have been my classmate,
might have walked the old neighborhood,
struggled with us, knew what work is.
I blinded myself to his history of privilege.
He'd been chained to a wall in the prison hut,
so why bow to this war criminal,
frail seer led to testify before Creon
while the Chorus in pink was ushered offstage?
The Chorus may have felt it savage, compassionless,
to hiss at the defender of détente, intervention,
hemisphere hegemony and overthrow—
once, the brain of Nixon, our blood line to the Hapsburgs—
for when the Senator spewed his regal curse,
no one spoke: they had defiled his hall,
its calm proceedings gave meaning,
an affront to Henry was a breach.
But the Senator hurt me, ratted my trust.
Not because he sicced his slick and frothing dogs,
but he whipped me with my own guilt,

that beautiful inward machine.
Pop indoctrination and other Media distractions
halted, the outraged Prisoner of War unmasked
as drone of the dictator class silent
the moment the Chorus whispered:
"War Crime War Crime War Crime."
Picture it: swept into the arms of the suited guard
the Code Pink girl rushes Henry,
shaking like Voodoo her shiny handcuffs,
the nauseated wife behind Schultz
flanked by two daughters in a trance.
The girl shoved away pumps above the wreckage
of Kissinger her scrawled sign: "Cambodia,"
the Senator cursing her, cursing all of us,
dredges up from his own inmost filth:
"Get out of here, you low-life scum."

5

I became all polymath love's androgynous advocate.

—William Faulkner

Revelatory

Always this inward thread plays over limestone and singing,
the blue dawn glacier breeze snaps at my face
downturned to a rare hummingbird in the cup of my right hand,
fingertips of the left pry clumsily among its plume to rescue the one flea.

Hapless

and dependent on a sacred way, religiously unbelieving,
who else expected it could turn out

by tricks of coincidence as immoderately nervous happiness?
To issue forth helpless
like a potted cactus, a slow formation with spines
greening in the wrong climate,

fictionalizes your own daylit fractal
might amount to any more than a fallen petal.

To see yourself blown off the windshield
by less than a breeze, mountainously
to elevate the lips and tongue your ravenous own inner life
gushes from—beyond hysteria,

is to call down the sisterly oracular vow keepers
and blue flame devotees.

In Defense of "Irony"

Once a solid slab on the kitchen's woodstove heated enough
to avoid scorched shirts, held by tongs before burnt handles
became non-conductive, now mostly plastic cases hot-wired
to flat aluminum. So, not iron. Ironic, pronounced
almost opposite the thing—which is said as *eye* and *earn*,
the fundamental capitalist principle, the jaw only slightly
involved juts lazily, the way the boss sucks down a whiskey
on his front porch while "irony" requires more involvement
on the part of the jaw not to mention the reminder
of physical activity as in "runny": like her nylon or my nose—
a jogger with jutting jawbone might say it, or a less than educated
workman might, in a flamboyant speech at strike or a march,
but who says it quickly, almost unsure, a foreign word
because in high school we lumped it into 'figures of speech'
(a phrase in itself meaning nothing and contradictory
as if ideas with physical bodies, a womanly *vavavaboom* out of
Sid Caesar could combine with an act of rhetorical sound).
So, you say it quickly and it sounds like science class *ion-y*
which fills the word with the northeastern accent that sets one apart,
although billionaires and at least one Royal do embed their remarks
with such elisions, lay effects of a bias toward labor
and away from the "treacherous upper classes"
who boil the hearts of the Left and the left behind.
Ironically ("r" a growl in the throat), iron in our souls,
precise thread mythic fates snip, spoken of most often
in postmortem, fits but awkwardly into the weave.
Personalities of enthroned rulers reappear after centuries
as our own indecisive presiders, pretenders like the previous dolt.
History contains a 14th c. regal set of jaw and the 21st
a squeamish use of accents to win over 'common man,' a posture,
evidence the candidate thinks himself small as you,
frail, in fact just a pussy, as he spurns the pressed
white shirt of his well-groomed, opponent.

And Et Cetera

The filly in a meadow is a dream.
Nightly, during the reign of the demagogue,
forecasters of the News like card sharks
shuffled and dealt opinions,
the filly in the meadow in a bluster of breezes,
and pushed the thread of a story uphill,
rolled away Floridian glacial till off his unkillable glitter.
Once I named my pickup Sisyphus Wrecks,
sharpened the clamps on its jumper cables,
filled and spit-shined a gas can,
pressed a nickel of air on the spare,
and onto the keychain, for luck,
I hooked my father's WWII dog tags.
Still, I pushed and towed the quiet relic up the hill,
the filly curious in the meadow, the radio on—
they were onto the new krypto-currency
usury then ("O Boy, Pound!" I said).
In the bluster of a breeze in the hemisphere of hysteria
we barter Covid shots for shreds of Confederate flags.
The past crawls out of an animal carcass.
There's no elaborate rewrite we survive.
A filly—in a meadow—it takes a body back.

Burn Moon August Six Twenty-Seventeen

Few palettes keep up.
Moonrise in night smoke.
Our eyes wear an impermanent cloak.
Scent of the Hunter, a clarity.
Skies on fire for the seventy-second year
since Hiroshima, beneath the Bear.
Moons rise—
Venus, The Dipper,
lost to our eyes.

Take Five

1.
Fifty years from now fourth graders will know.
Stalin, Mao, Idi, Truman, Jim Jones
they'll forget, but what Hitler did, they'll know.
It's hard to say history's tablet shines:
steps up the temple shimmer and fade too.
Antiquity fades—abracadabra
the busts of armless Venus, and Plato,
Socrates, Alexander—all sell Vodka
or Buicks, Scholarships, Freedom or flight,
then swim into starlight's perishing night.
As everyone collapses in thin burnt
atmosphere, he scuttles along cement
sticky with blood, and we flee or go blind.

2.
Government shrunk to the size of an insect,
I unlaced my boot to squash it with the heel,
but nostalgic for old Khrushchev's shoe—
I laughed at his old joke: "We will bury you"
and the government bit me on the toe.
Then scurried up a book on Congressional sex,
slinked behind gold embroidered curtains, real
Confederate statuary, and a Peace Prize,
jetted the snout of a bull at whose sneeze
government transformed to the air we breathe.
So I stood up, swung Old Hickory by the hilt
(rifled from a batting cage at seventh inning stretch)
and strode off, handcuffs jangling at my belt,
off to hunt the government, that cockroach.

3. *Gabriel, the Angel*
I was born the day Jesus was conceived.
I was gold as a lake in her window,
filthy wings much too large—she didn't mind.
Kneeling, the sun pooled in her lap, that blue
you always see dappled with soil and mist.
If you think my brief task in this story
a simple one, you underestimate
freedom: hers, and mine. I stepped through the dust
and brought the message, this awkward body
a part of the plan for the stream of lit
water to pour in. My lovely peasant
made a man of me too: I walked off then,
wings dry as maple leaves, a message sent,
I wander earth now, me the go-between.

4.
We who have pieces puzzle the Berlin Wall,
flying them in to fit the jigsaw,
to put it all back together again.
Artists, we step back to relish its flaw.
We who have jarred up the volcanic ash,
now with our last breath withering, we cast
it to outer space. I'm only afraid
of everything, repenting what's unsaid.
The act, waging in my dull brain, is sin
only if undone. I wish I could lean
where the sprouted buttercups have broken
over the chipped wall I've so often seen
you beside, drowsy, as we all are now:
they can turn our throats golden if we bow.

5.
The cap goes back on the tip of my pen
giving up, failed to find utterly still
the few sun-up chickadees who mangle
our suet globs, wince at a flicker's perch
of a Monday morning too bright even
for ridgetop hawks' aching wingtips to stretch
what's meaningless across what's breathless
and skate the gloss bay blue light of no wave
where frigid engine clatter doesn't miss
what lights an immovable grove or give
vanishing shy goldfinches a way out
or harrowing woodpecker in soap light
light that won't resist my happy failures
to sing yes yes what's not human matters.

Of Myself I Sing

Another poet murdered for apostasy,
Mohammad Bashir al-Aani along with his son Elyas,
this time by Isis, and Dareen Tatour
imprisoned for a resistance poem and a post—
"You look like a terrorist," they said
when they broke into her home in the dark of night,
and, long after death, Mahmoud Darwish, who
wrote in youth against the Occupier,
disparaged now by Defense Minister of Occupation
long since the line in his I.D. poem raged,
"the flesh of the occupier will be my sustenance."
Who in my country will sing so dangerously?

Pharaoh's Dance

1.
After a cloud pearls away, I become afraid
of what was bequeathed on that elegant height,
my father's missions among the gunners.

A shape like anything else, memory in its imp shreds
of black and white, the flotilla dissolves.

Daylight does this trick with likenesses,
but not cloud work at night.

Mudflats gray and sopping splendor under a torch
where, humorless, the farting midget Satan leads—
behind Virgil's dyspeptic sneer, and young Dante planted his foot.

2.
When you drove down that street and
had to stop for the light,
women with loud offers
would shout in your window
and with swelling teeth and lips
simulate the mechanism
by which to invite you
until the light changed—
writhing blue tank tops in the rearview.

3.
Outside of luck
is the dampening scream—snapped twigs,
their escaping leaves in a hurry
climb onto frenzied verandas
where shouting out the names in wonder
the onslaught begins,
clothes hanging off a line,
iron with clothespins in her teeth
to signal a pause, the little bell.

4.
An orange wandering the table,
another lifted onto the plate.
Light captures this.

Gifts of percussive wind, the
uppity nobody,
the one with the wobbly trumpet
blazing out his eyes.

5.
When she was turning into the light
he thought he understood his place on earth—
the same as blades of grass, a stump of tree,
this monument to a duplicitous political hero,
its shadow exactly aligned,
the sun's digitized angles circularly fanned
over our hemisphere
absorbed by this movement around and
around how many the
                precise number
of mysteries left captioned
as events in albums we
peruse politely asking
Who's that one? What
was her name?

6.
 When equinox brushes the ridgeline the
last of winter tips the firs,
night pools in the valley whose
ridges tell direction—
here is the disappearance of celebrity.
After dark seeps from grass blade,
bone twines inverted root,

and the insane reach through branches.
Crisp last light along ridge tops,
belief in the faraway vanishes,
and, candles doused—night floats uphill
before ascendant thought: light even lighter,
in peaks, on moon, a sudden fading after
starlight, before memory,
a pool of first thought.

Letter to Sam Hamill from Boston, 1979

The third renovation in a row the crew walked off today.
Nothing gets finished, "just abandoned," but the job leaves splinters.
Lifting a stout at *The Plough*, your name came up.
Tim read a poem about quitting this hardhat economy
by a guy from the Tetons: frozen fenceposts and the usual—
snow-hard compost, woodsmoke,
a line from time to time that missed the beat,
too long in the rhythms of the trades.

The body beside me sleeps like a machine.
Breath noises, inward murmur, a moan within the dream.
Romance the illusion of the mirror, Cocteau's door to hell,
who cares about Eurydice?
                         We can't ever quite come to rest.
In a photo of Auden's face cigarette smoke blurs all those creases,
a river's unraveling away from rope.

I won't describe the face I saw tonight on the subway.
Hours later I'm still confused, and ashamed.
We're anonymous enough out here, but this face
charred by all our poisons—I forced my eyes to believe
we were born in the same place, drink the same water,
run a palm across the same chrome and granite.
In the rattling seats, most of us show no longing.
A creased brow and I look toward the window
where my own face blackens, passing underground,
brake-lights flowering on the tunnel wall.
When the train lurches, I get out and walk into the city
—a thin Vietnamese in woman's slippers
shivers in the draft below a vent.
Not far away a heaven's made from turrets and old tiles—
the perishable order of doorways, a man asleep on a stoop
where someone's hand placed a withered carrot.

Past shadow and streetlight at the quarry entrance,
slate and granite veined, whorled, chopped, routed
and eroded by a stream, or shoe and wheel
these roads of lichen, algae, oldest mosses, oak and bowers of elm.
In Munich, Achenbach, before he fell in love
as the boy ushered him toward death
passed a place like this and smelled the coming war.
Headstones harvested here line up blank.
To me, a young and foolish optimist, they're shouting,
"We resist, we resist, we resist you."

I was a boy full of milk and loved the wind
veering down a street a mile from here.
The summer my hand took form from an arrow,
pines fanned one another in a field.
My forearm sore from the bowstring,
the first shots fell into New Hampshire,
but then grinded one after another unlike any bird,
twanged against a straw bag of bullseyes.
A hawk above the boughs brushed small loops of haze.

I'm not sure why I wrote you this letter.
I walked in black fields where the eyes of animals hid from me.
"Nostalgia," Rexroth said in that way he has
of instilling syllables as if carving them on a maple
whose leaves in the clear basin beside his camp
sing the history of every word. But it's not that.

Try this—I'm driving with the family on a typical Thursday.
Passing a lake, I want to have a look.
My grandmother objects, but I pull over anyway
and the noises stop, no ripples—
a birch stand fills with dusk, sky turns to chalk.
I set the bow—how green this lichen.
Fieldstone walls have served a hundred families,

each more indifferent than the rest,
but I draw the bow, can't waste a shot,
arrow feathers leave my hand,
the shaft disappears then, bone white,
arcs over the hawk's tail
and falls back down to me,
craning my neck to watch.

Lucretius, an Interpretation

De Rerum Natura IV, 1015-1057

It's not so different from being awake— and it's magnificent
a man's mind can kill even while dreaming of Greatness—
we carry on, equally committed though asleep;
a politician dreams of defeat—imprisoned,
he's in a brawl or knife fight,
and cries out his throat was hacked.
Many asleep might roar out of the depths
mangled in the jaws of a lion, or a furious cougar,
so loud do their howls fill the bed chamber.
Many, talking in sleep, boast about themselves,
only to bellow the truth and prove they're liars.
Many die, many feel their real bodies
plunge off a ridge into the ground,
and awaken in terror, minds clanking in chains
and don't recognize their own twisted corpses.

It's the same for a dreamer beside
a mellow spring who, very thirsty,
inhales a river whole.
Little boys asleep beside a dripping jug
or a rising lake, raise their nighties
and wet the bed soaking precious Babylonian quilts
with all the pee such a body can store in a day.
Later, as young men in the riptides of semen,
every growth spurt purges flesh,
they encounter exotic bodies on the street,
images spark a voluptuous bloom
to enlarge their already bursting seed,
an erection beyond human wishes
plumes out of control,
floods the mind, soaks their clothes.

It disturbs us, I've already mentioned, this seed,
when limbs articulated in young adulthood solidify,
for one leads to commotion in the other, and excites;
from a man comes a seed only man can issue;
before sperm leaves its source,
wreaking limb and joint to spurt off the body,
it gathers in tested neural sockets to emerge
doubly boomed in boy genitals.
Stroking such pockets of seed swells them,
desire ejaculates where intensity aims—
wherever the body points, the mind is love's wound;
all men fall for it, just as in close combat
when the blow strikes, blood gushes, reddens the enemy,
so, hit with Venus's spear shaped as a boy's
pretty leg or as a woman throbbing
in molten heat, in whichever form her spear arises,
he dances and runs riot like a stream's downhill torrent
to lay with first one body, then another, and another—
blunt lust races bliss.

Autobiography of the Last Monarch Butterfly

to the memory of Ron Schreiber

*You are entrusted to the eternal keeping
that preserves a butterfly's trace in the air*
—Czeslaw Milosz

*... noi siam vermi
nati al formar l'angelica farfalla*

*... born worms
who sculpt the angelic butterfly*
—Dante Alighieri

Where I Was
When she asked me to wear her silk underpants,
I knew it couldn't last.
Two months and she was with another
grease monkey she met in the bare neighborhood bar
shaved her blond head, armloads of tattoos, a taste for heroin.
Two years later I was near homeless.
Junkies in Albuquerque stole my pack.
Dusty and thirsty, I sat on a curb on Boylston Street.
She didn't recognize me.
Her face was the cover of *Vogue* when she strode past. Beatific—that kind
of beauty, it had to come back.
What came back was the night she threw a knife at my door.
Police or ambulance sirens went off two blocks away.
No one said a word.

Soul Bubbling
My sandals began to weaken outside Denver.
On a little wooden bridge,
I burned up every picture and number holding me.
Ashes in the toe, I danced barefoot in puddles
and handed off my last dollars.

By morning I sat on that outcrop
above a stream pouring stars.
I was carried through North America
like wooden Christ on a spear.
The shadow of my wings fell over
the cities and I moved on.
They offered me at truck stops,
on the corners of fly-past streets
as if unusual air hovered round me,
my backpack imbued with intelligence.
I was a tree in the wilderness without will
and swayed like a boxer in the dirty rest-stop mirror,
my beat mug a shelled walnut.
I arose from the embryo of a tent and walked away.
left my face in a field with a crumpled umbrella—
another self, thug of daylight, stalked me.
I was prying his fingers off the side of the boat
when it came to me, underwater, a soul bubbling
out of deserted lips as I held him under.

Men with Blankets
Out the café window
a man in a ripped Hawaiian shirt, faded flowers,
sprints across the street,
twists his head, arm arcing the last wine
out a green bottle, and spatters
the label tossing it in the dumpster,
his tongue a shocking red,
face compliant, almost tired of duties,
buttoning his shirt like an athlete leaving the field.
The reservoir's mirror dances behind him.

A white-haired man, in his boxer shorts,
very thin with sacks of tattooed breasts,
lunges toward a jogger, coughs,

bending so he almost falls,
face red between the shaft of quivering knees,
the elastic of his underwear
drooped past his wretched haunch.
I can't take my eyes away,
handed a coffee and change.

The man in the flowered shirt lays him down on the bench,
pulls a quilt up to his shoulder, drapes it, smooths it.
Sits there till the old man lies still.
Wind riffles the reservoir, dust picks up.
He stretches, stands to bum a smoke,
is refused and walks along the avenue.

Great Oblivion
In the tomb of the job spinning a shroud.
When the hawk like a kite slices the slough.
Money, hair, dust and ash,
feathers lost and the fragments of poems washed
in the stream black as the heavens, as human filth,
a splinter in your eye,
flake of my life.

On its unmapped course,
budding and flowering and seeding
the empty pot by the door in the air,
what passes curves this way,
saunters down the hall in the school of madness.

Black fingernails caressing headphones,
the survivor knots and unknots a rope.
Black raincoat, silk hair,
a child, no more than a child,
wobbles his small bike over snow on the railroad tracks,
rolls down the grade, leans over handlebars,

and weaves his bald front tire
into the iced puddle.

Boxes of bones in the trunks of dented cars
rattled over potholes for weeks
and the gauchos who can't drive
kept stopping too fast
which made the bones gnash their teeth
and grumble the ride
to the dentist of gravel is white as sand
longing to lose the sunlight
forever in earth's quilted windows

Lost Magic
When an hour of Harleys growls through Skagit County
for the Oyster Run, every earring, lip ring, nipple ring pulls
its patch of flesh forward, magnets draw the body down
to Highway Nine or on the porch with a cat named Gramma.
Meanwhile in the living room, Boeing's newest jet
stuck up near the roof of sound,
the family believes in apocalyptic beards
without smiles or names or gasoline.

Where I Come From
When there was a narrative, I was still a boy
catching all the meanings my adults could hint.
But who were you, inventors of the story?
Which constellations did you interpret to devolve a job of work?
In blood-smeared robe, a meataxe in hand,
the butcher smiles across the counter;
a mound of coin shimmers at dawn,
she empties a black-frilled apron on the kitchen table;
turquoise car to the exotic sea, warm and away from here,
top-down cruiser, radio on Sinatra;
lapping sea in weeds where current skims high flood below a bridge,

naiads or nymphs whose crab pots would mount the walls of Ilium
and this tawdry fish-stank porch,
sons and daughters of lobstermen swim there,
bawling in the noon sun, in iodine, in hope,
what studs the rush tide made them dive to be—
Did you ever know better?
In the sea of sweat, workers and coworkers,
class of the broad vowel and stepped on phoneme
hang on sacks of grain, a broken loose cargo
wrapped in human sinew and tattoo
of prole art running up her ankle and calf,
vein and coil along her thigh, scroll work
of an indolent scribbler who knew all about toil
and embroidered our flesh
before sending us off to sea.

Dark home under the soil
In one hour, this city—and the subway is Arachne—
feverishly threads the heart, a severed obstacle.
Stuck in transit we leer at the bodies of the others.
A madwoman spits tobacco juice in your face
she's carried twenty miles away in ten minutes.

Days pass like gum into the ground.
Where a body fell, high windows overlook the city,
a spark from the plane's empty window seat.

Two working men shout their life stories
the stenographer with beaded chain dangling eyeglasses
foregoes the evening paper gets it all down
no detail falls to unrecorded time.

All didactic we head south across the river
rented sails in afternoon humidity
{"Can you actually read that ...Chicken scratch?"

she asks, falling into the seat next to my elbow
weighed down by immense envelopes of x-ray negatives
corrupting the vision she recalls
her only son's body wiped from her eyes.}
hung from chrome subway bars they tell the train
simple truths of child-rearing—their sons scuttle on spongy sea legs,
elbows out, larger girth, shy but equal to the talk—
TV commercials the template for advice
bright green shirt, smudged knee.

A woman, once lovely, once everybody's baby doll,
fights over money with her daughter, nine years old
"Shut up! This is fair!"
"No, it's not."
The humility it takes or lack of self-effacement
not to hide you always abuse her
distinguishes one class from another
on that other line air-conditioning always works
swelter of June the poor ride hot
and they are loud
venture anywhere
ask anything indiscreet impersonal
they give you the thoroughly smug.

Across the rocking, two salesmen, smoke on the breath,
a black man missing front teeth in tie and starch
white Mentor, cigarette tucked
neat behind his ear, greased hair.

We're figuring it out.
In our proper suits we go to school.
What you have, that's for me.
What I have, it's off Mass Ave.

6

*It is not good to forget over what gulfs the spirit
of the beauty of humanity, the petal of a lost flower blown seaward
by the night-wind, floats to its quietness.*

—Robinson Jeffers, *"Apology for Bad Dreams"*

Cells

for Molly Louzan

1.
In pasture lands of old New Jersey, monthly on Sundays,
I wedged between a niche and a post at the Bursar's offices.

Allotted telephone minutes as if "what hath god wrought"
were a miracle, I told her, up in our northern snow, that,
though in middling health, I intended to stick with my calling.

Over itchy feedback, occasional varied Eastern Seaboard
or New York boroughs' accents cackling over high squeals,
her breathy conspiring voice hushed me, "Shush. Party line."

Not as in a "falling in step with," or "living unquestioningly according to,"
"accepting criteria to judge a good life, happily married,"
but *of the neighborhood* when she'd say, "Is another party on the line?"

Today we might wonder: "Oh-oh, you're cutting out,"
or "Am I losing you?" or, more provocatively,
"Oh, are you gone or am I in a dead zone?"

2.
Dead winter, a foot of snow on the fire-escape,
the bleakest night all month in the downtown Yakima lobby,
gurneys hauled overdosed carcasses to the street.

Crippled bikers' chains scraped the marble stairs.
Country twang scratched like cracked paint behind the doors.
Very thin women measured drops into pale vials.

I carted my wounds, and my typewriter
to room 11-A, where a worn quilt was mine as long as I wanted,
and where a cowboy's heel scraped the hall's creaking floor,
came to a standstill—the moment filled with snow, with ice.

Then a thud, and silence; a more considered knock
cranked up my alarm. But his yellow thumb extended
"*From the desk of...*" on a Post-it scribbled with her number,
and a man with a few teeth rasped, "Call your mother."

3.
Rationed phone chatter
and the art lost now of letter-writing
were all the contact we had.

Unlike this morning, my sister's voice through the cell,
that claw to the left of my brain.
Within seconds I wince, my elbow torqued, and press "speaker."

It always blares—prying neighbors turn just so
and become party to my grief, "She's gone."
And my rote but deeply felt, "Goodbye, I love you."

4.
Our phone calls, it was my luck,
filled me utterly with her voice,
which for reasons left mysterious
she cultivated as if she were a product
of early television, of that pop mist
which had evoked through model-shoots
in checkered two-piece bathing suits
a not-so-subtle postwar lust.
Her voice answering was breathless,
as if it carried Hollywood's caress
like an invitation in her mere
"Hello-o, who is it?" and never
or barely ever on the third ring,
nor so formal as, "Whom shall I say is calling?"

5.
Of an age anticipating fame might ring up any housewife,
her cadence was nuanced even at ninety-three
on the last bed by that last window beside those last
hedges blocking her view of SUV hearses, delivery vans, and ambulance.

She endeared herself to no less than ten uniformed kind ladies
among whom an Angel of Death I thought
need not have had so childlike a countenance or lilt
to apply morphine to my mind not liberally enough to quell travail.

Yet, aware and not aware, she summoned an indwelling
to the mouthpiece on her granddaughter's cell
and invited us, who stood or sat or held on
around her deathbed, to joke about her "sexy voice."

Teatime

       of a winter evening is when
the mauve light bores down on Mount Erie
while to sugarcoat Sugarloaf's hump
the truculent ghost of moonrise
cranks upward, damp, filthy, translucent
through a mask of axle-greased silk
and before I'm halfway through my cup of tea
pea soup boils up from the soggy forest
onto the shoulders of these hills
which shrug off a drenched meadow
and the world vanishes into sheepskin fog,
but the moon keeps on climbing,
a milky cataract in the frayed wool sky.

Bird Count on Back Roads

Near Thomas Road, crossing the valley,
I spot three young eagles
perched on a cottonwood limb
when the heron, startled, swerves up—
its cracked cry—
my first thought: *Man Kills Great Blue with Pickup*—but up
she rises and unfolds above this morning's
flash and turn of a hundred dunlins,
then all quiet,
a white rushing creek.

Next day, ducks float in flooded potato fields,
two ring-tails—a sparrow hawk or a kestrel, I don't know
the smaller raptors—
klatches of snow geese in vast grime,
a living oxymoron:
their white handkerchiefs out
to purify the muck.
One more annoyed heron
flaps away in uplifting displeasure.

Days later, spattered with the sugar
fed to our precious Anna's humming duo, new snow
dusts the suet for towhees,
amused chickadees, bushtits by the dozens;
the ruby-lipped Northern Flicker couple
flung orange wings in snowdrifts
at gray squirrels fat as porcupine,
one ground squirrel
all business
chased another.

I remember the drive the morning of Christmas Eve
raven splurged white moon shine,
his wide caw soared over wet Thomas,
a cat-like goshawk or merlin
poised every few miles
between pollarded lindens
on rain-shimmering barbwire,
a hundred ducks rode shotgun
to a lake of rain
newly spilled onto uprooted stalks,
two or three hundred swan
spotless as first communion dresses,
legs tarred black
as my Christmas coal stocking.

Farther north
two of the balds hunch on a branch
above a drainage
and the same slim heron as yesterday, today or tomorrow
over Chuckanut's estuary
where, proud and fattened, a young
eagle surveys from the crown of a willow—
or is he a golden—
dawn stunned in a field where once a thousand
or so many uncountable trumpeters
taught celestial happiness to a school of amphibians
forgotten now
in this lively mud.

1957, Paragon Park

> *Every poem an epitaph, and any action*
> *Is a step toward the block, to the fire, down the sea's throat*
> *Or to an illegible stone; and that is where we start.*
> —T. S. Eliot, "*Little Gidding*"

Carry me back into open daylight the way
I carry now one summer evening's end of the season
when the swaying Giant Roller Coaster shut down;
we were to sit by ourselves, my sister and I,
      beside the open bar room doors:
            fried clams, Cokes,
our beach wishes flung off the waves;
four low quiet voices—
      two men in Scally caps, wives
whispering: my sweet aunt Mae, always in whispers—
faces and gestures fixed in memory:
the owners of the beach-time cocktail bar, her friends;
our two 'children plates'
      by the starlit doorway, chair legs upturned
at all the other tables: ages ten and seven—
white sand, salt white beach, "Hush," she said, "Hush" again,
from those sad creaking barstools:
clink of glasses, ring of cigar smoke, the fryer's sizzle—
I'm back there now,
though the ground's scraped bare and the insult
of a bricked-up plaza buried the sea,
wind and sand choked their lungs,
      cancers' surprise ending
           to good, true friendship
                when whispering,
closing night of their final summer's run,
the kindly beach in every way their own,
crests above the sparking sand, gull screech, cool shade.
Do I make too much of one summer evening?
I changed my life, but I've carried them

half a century—their gentle, intense goodbyes—
into open daylight, another 'now,'
not so different from this.

NOTE

"War Crimes" is built on an event the reader may locate on the internet by using the final line of the poem. The cover photo is one of several taken at that event. The article recounts an incident that disturbed many Americans in which Senator McCain, who was later revered for his opposition to the fascistic takeover of the White House and Congress as he was dying of brain cancer, insulted and denied the rights of citizens who entered a Senate Armed Services Committee meeting, to protest McCain, committee chair who invited as advisor Henry Kissinger, "who enabled dictators, extended the Vietnam War, laid the path to the Khmer Rouge killing fields, stage-managed a genocide in East Timor, overthrew the democratically elected left-wing government in Chile and encouraged Nixon to wiretap his political adversaries (*The Intercept* 2016)." I thank Harvard's 1994 Summer Symposium on Lucretius & Epicurus for stimulating my interest in both, and Stephen Greenblatt's *The Swerve: How the World Became Modern* for reawakening it.

ABOUT THE AUTHOR

Michael Daley was born and raised in Dorchester, Massachusetts. He holds a B.A. from the University of Massachusetts and an M.F.A. from the University of Washington. His work has been awarded by Seattle Arts Commission, Washington State Arts Commission, Massachusetts Cultural Council, Fessenden Foundation, National Endowment of the Humanities, Fulbright, The Skagit River Poetry Foundation, and The Poets House Trust. A retired teacher, he lives near Deception Pass in Washington.

www.ingramcontent.com/pod-product-compliance
Lightning Source LLC
Chambersburg PA
CBHW022156080426
42734CB00006B/452